To Dave.

WALSALL
THROUGH TIME
Michael Glasson

Best wishes,

Mike Glasson

AMBERLEY PUBLISHING

For my parents

First published 2011

Amberley Publishing
Cirencester Road, Chalford,
Stroud, Gloucestershire GL6 8PE

www.amberleybooks.com

Copyright © Michael Glasson 2011

The right of Michael Glasson to be identified as the
Author of this work has been asserted in accordance
with the Copyrights, Designs and Patents Act 1988.

ISBN 978-1-84868-748-6

British Library Cataloguing in Publication Data.
A catalogue record for this book is available from
the British Library.

Typeset in 9.5pt on 12pt Celeste.
Typesetting by Amberley Publishing.
Printed in the UK.

Introduction

The modern streets of Walsall, with their mix of nineteenth- and twentieth-century architecture, give few hints of any antiquity. Yet Walsall is a lot older than many people realise. Although the first undisputed documentary reference to the town is not until 1159, it seems likely that, as Dr Steve Bassett has recently argued, Walsall's ancient parish church of St Matthew originated as a minster foundation in Saxon times. Other scholars have argued that the *walh* element in the town's name may be a Saxon reference to a Celtic-British or 'welsh' presence. This interpretation has been disputed, but what is certain is that a charter giving the right to hold weekly markets in Walsall was granted in 1220, and by the fourteenth century we have evidence of a flourishing urban community with the right to appoint its own mayors and burgesses, and the valuable privilege of being exempt from certain feudal duties and charges. Walsall's role as a self-governing place where goods could be exchanged or sold thus stretches back over 700 years, and the town's role as a place where things are manufactured goes back nearly as far. Iron ore and coal were being dug as early as 1300 and records of surnames such as Spurrier (or spur-maker) and Brazier (worker in brass) suggest that the town's history of metalworking dates back at least to the fourteenth century. By the time of the Tudors, the town was specialising in the manufacture of bits and other horse goods, for which it was later to become so celebrated.

Of the medieval and early modern Walsall – the home of the English Civil War hero Colonel Tinker Fox and a place once visited by John Wesley – few physical traces now remain. For this we largely have to thank the spectacular expansion and rebuilding of the town after 1800. During the nineteenth century the population of the borough grew almost ninefold, to nearly 90,000. From 1847 Walsall had its own station, and the arrival of the railways heralded massive growth in the town's leather and metal trades, which developed international trading links throughout the British Empire and beyond. By the end of Queen Victoria's reign, Walsall could claim to be 'the town of a hundred trades' and the greatest centre of saddlery and harness manufacture in Europe.

Victorian rebuilding was followed by twentieth-century slum clearance, which brought about the destruction of the many unhealthy and overcrowded yards and closes of the town. Clearance of the once highly picturesque Church Hill, with its network of narrow winding streets and alleys, left St Matthew's church stranded in a sea of emptiness. Much greater destruction to the historic character of the town followed in the 1960s as planners and developers set about giving Walsall a modern town centre. The historic High Street, praised by John Betjeman for its attractiveness, was brutally transformed into what a subsequent council publication described as 'a bleak soulless open space [which] has given planning a bad name locally'. Elsewhere, tower blocks were erected, which cast the surrounding neighbourhoods into deep shadow. Lessons were learned and during the 1980s and '90s conservation areas were designated and a number of important historic buildings were restored and adapted for new use, the White Hart in Caldmore, the Guildhall, and St Paul's church among them. A number of excellent modern buildings – human in scale and incorporating traditional materials such as brick and tile – were erected, of which Rushall Mews and the Darwall Street branch of Lloyds TSB are good examples.

If the photographs in this book demonstrate that there has been a great deal of destruction to the historic character of the town and that too many of the new developments are bland and lacking in personality, I hope it will also show that much remains to explore. If much of the town centre is, to quote one authority, 'humdrum or downright poor', Walsall is still a place with a distinct identity and traditions, and a strong feeling of continuity. Unlike so many British towns, it remains a place where real things are made. In often inconspicuous backstreet factories it is still possible to find highly skilled metal and leatherworkers making superb saddles for the Household Cavalry, turbochargers for Porsches and handbags for export to Japan. St Matthew's church still dominates Church Hill, and Walsall market continues to be held in the town centre, as it has been every week since 1220.

Walsall's Tram Service
Locally brewed Highgate Mild is advertised on the side of a tram in this atmospheric photograph of around 1930. The days of Walsall's trams were numbered, and the last service was converted to a trolleybus route in October 1933.

Market (High St.), Walsall.

Walsall High Street

The town's ancient High Street, climbing steadily to St Matthew's church and built on a curve, was described by Sir John Betjeman in 1959 as potentially 'one of the most attractive streets in England', lined with 'charming and modest' buildings. Within ten years of Betjeman's comments nearly every building had been bulldozed.

St Matthew's Church
Standing at nearly 500 feet above sea level, St Matthew's is Walsall's ancient parish church. The elegant spire is a conspicuous local landmark. Its exposed location means that frequent repair is necessary. The author's ancestor Thomas Mold donated ten pence towards its rebuilding in 1669. Redevelopment of the High Street in the 1960s had a disastrous impact on the relationship of the church to the town, and even the most ardent fan of 1960s architecture would find it hard to make a case for the Overstrand, which wrecks the classic view up the High Street.

St Matthew's Church (Interior)

The church was largely rebuilt in 1819–21. Francis Goodwin, the architect, used cast iron for the columns and window frames and timber and plaster for the charming fan vault. The choir houses the finest set of medieval misericords to be found in Staffordshire. It is rare to find misericords in a parish church and tradition has it that they were rescued from Halesowen Abbey (whose abbot was patron of Walsall church) at the time of the Dissolution.

Church Hill from the Air
Walsall market is in progress in the
foreground of this view, which dates from
around 1930. Behind the church spire,
Hill Street can be seen winding its way
towards Birmingham Road, and Springhill
Road in the background (completed as a
shortcut in 1914) still looks very raw. The
lower image shows the oldest part of the
church, the inner crypt, with its beautiful
thirteenth-century ribbed vaulting.

The Leathern Bottle

This ancient pub stood opposite the south door of St Matthew's church, on the corner of Temple Street. Its name was perhaps intended as a reference to the town's famous leather-working trade, since the neighbouring streets housed many saddlers and harness-makers. The lamp of another pub, the Barley Mow, can just be seen behind the Leathern Bottle. All of these buildings were demolished as part of the council's slum-clearance programme, although the foundation stone of the Church House, which once stood on the opposite corner of Temple Street, has been preserved. (*Photograph right courtesy of Stan Hill*)

Hill Street

The steeply sloping Hill Street linked Church Hill in the foreground with Birmingham Road. In the early twentieth century it was still crowded with houses and pubs; the sign of the original Queen's Head can be glimpsed on the right-hand side of the photograph. These picturesque (if insanitary) buildings were swept away after 1930 and the residents moved to newly built council estates. Today Hill Street is just a memory. (*Photograph above courtesy of Stan Hill*)

New Street

It is hard to believe that the steep, winding route of New Street was once frequented by coaching traffic. The tightly clustered three-storey houses and shops along its route were a feature of the Walsall skyline until their eventual demolition. Today only a fragment of New Street remains. (*Photograph above courtesy of Stan Hill*)

Dudley Street

This was another of the narrow, winding streets that once radiated from Church Hill. The timber-framed building on the right is the Duke of York pub, probably a medieval structure, which was demolished in 1937. The patriotic occasion recorded here is thought to be the Silver Jubilee of King George V in 1935. Today this is a busy section of the inner relief road. (*Photograph above courtesy of Stan Hill*)

Church Steps

This remarkable early photograph, probably dating from the mid-1850s, shows the steps below St Matthew's church. The tracery of the church windows can just be seen at the top of the photograph. Until 1852, the 'market cross' and stocks stood near here. The shops at the foot of the steps include the boot- and shoe-making business of Ann Betts. The area was cleared in the 1950s to create the gardens seen today. (*Photograph above courtesy of Stan Hill*)

Walsall High Street (I)

This view is from the top of the High Street towards Digbeth, an area that formed the core of the medieval market town. Many of the attractive and unpretentious buildings that lined the street probably preserved the dimensions of the medieval burgage plots. Today only a handful of these buildings survive, fortunately including the characterful Guildhall, which was rescued from demolition by local architect Gordon Foster.

Walsall High Street (II)

This view from the High Street towards Digbeth includes the Carlton Hotel on the left with its elegant (probably early-eighteenth-century) cupola and the Woolpack Inn in the middle distance. These were both demolished in the 1960s along with most of their neighbours. The Green Dragon, on the right-hand side of the photograph, is one of Walsall's oldest recorded inns and, happily, has survived.

The Woolpack Inn

This inn stood at the corner of Old Square and Digbeth until 1892. It was a fine example of half-timbering, and its picturesque appearance made it a popular subject for Victorian artists. A much-loved replacement with imitation half-timbering, Ye Olde Woolpack, was in turn demolished in 1964 to make way for the bland Old Square shopping precinct.

Digbeth

The name 'Digbeth' is first recorded in 1583 and is thought to mean 'dyke pool'. The remarkable four-storey gabled building seen here probably had sixteenth-century origins. By the date of this photograph (pre-1876), it had fallen on hard times and was providing cheap lodgings. It was demolished in 1892 to make way for a shopping arcade. (*Photograph right courtesy of John Griffiths*)

THE BRIDGE, WALSALL.

The George Hotel (I)

Walsall's town square takes its name from a long-vanished bridge over the Walsall Brook, a tributary of the River Tame. In the Middle Ages the town mill was situated here. By the late nineteenth century the space was surrounded by impressive buildings, including the George Hotel with its fine Ionic portico. The George had been built in 1781, and in its heyday it was a celebrated coaching inn, with stabling for 150 horses.

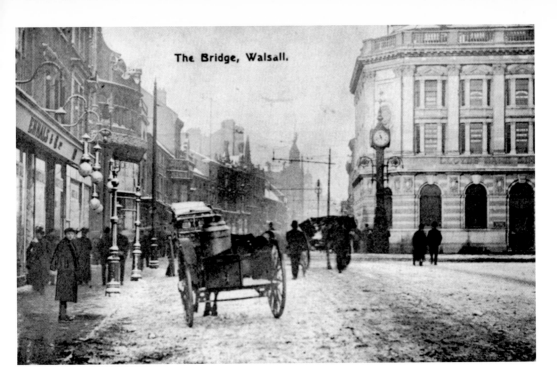

The Bridge, Walsall.

Messrs Ennals' Stores

A milk cart waits in the snow outside Messrs Ennals' stores on the Bridge in this postcard sent from 'Min' to her friend 'Emley' in 1907. The exotic rooflines of the Grand Theatre and Her Majesty's Theatre can be seen in the distance.

The Bridge, Looking West
Sister Dora surveys the waiting trams in this peaceful scene from the 1920s. In recent years the Bridge has been redeveloped as the Civic Square.

The Bridge, Looking North

Trams wait on the Bridge in this late-1920s view. Walsall's trams were gradually replaced by trolleybuses and motorbuses and the last tram ran in 1933. Among the buildings in the background are the Dora Café and Ennals, outfitters and house furnishers. The Ennals family produced some notable individuals including the Labour peer David Ennals (Baron Ennals).

Sister Dora's Memorial, The Bridge

Sister Dora is one of the most respected figures in Walsall's history. Born Dorothy Pattison, she came to Walsall in 1865 and set about transforming standards of nursing care in the Cottage Hospital. Her role as a nursing pioneer makes her a figure of national significance, and her early death in 1878 left the town stunned. Francis Williamson's fine memorial reflects the great regard in which she was held. A group of nurses is seen here in 1948 continuing the tradition of nursing care in the town.

The Bridge, Walsall.

The Bridge

This Edwardian view of the Bridge has a wonderful air of peace and stillness. Among the landmarks are the *Observer* offices, the George Hotel, and the entrance to the recently erected Digbeth arcade.

The George Hotel (II)

Walsall's finest 1930s building was the George Hotel, opened in November 1935 as a replacement for the porticoed building seen in previous photographs. It was described at the time as being 'the most up to date hotel in the Midlands'. Its refined, minimalist Art Deco design did not save it from being demolished in 1979. The clock on the left of the upper image was affectionately known locally as the four-faced liar, as each face was said to give a different time.

Lower Bridge Street, Walsall.

Bridge Street, Looking East

The upper photograph shows Bridge Street in a transitional stage. The corporation decided that such a major thoroughfare needed to be wider, and between 1918 and 1932 the south side of the street was demolished piecemeal. The picture house on the right of the photograph, opened in 1920, forms part of the new frontage. Recent additions to the scene include the *Source of Ingenuity* fountain by sculptor Tom Lomax, installed in 2001.

Bridge Street

The north side of Bridge Street was untouched by the road widening seen in the previous photograph, and despite one or two modern intrusions, it retains much of its late-Victorian character. Many of the buildings have fine architectural details and the former Taylor's Music Warehouse of 1891 (with the prominent gable) is ornamented with busts of the great composers and figures of musicians carrying tiny bronze instruments.

Walsall Bus Station

The bus station opened in 1935, on the former site of the Bluecoat School. Its dramatic replacement, designed by Alford Hall Monaghan Morris architects, opened in 2001. The attractive neo-Georgian offices of the previous bus station were retained and have recently been refurbished.

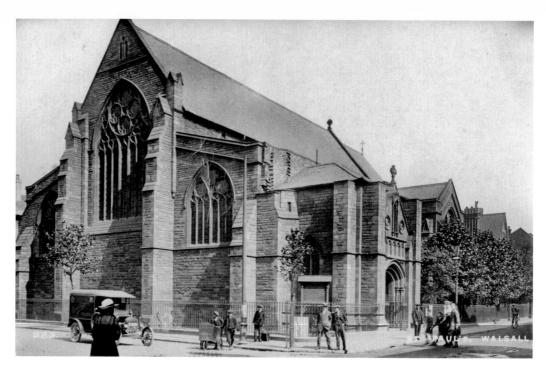

St Paul's Church (The Crossing)

Designed by John Loughborough Pearson, the celebrated architect of Truro Cathedral, St Paul's church was lavishly built with beautiful fittings and superb stained glass, although Pearson's proposed spire was never built. By the 1980s the congregation had dwindled and the church was in need of a new purpose. It was imaginatively converted in the early 1990s to incorporate meeting rooms, shops, a café and a chapel. New entrances were opened onto St Paul's Street.

Park Street (1)

Once the route to the Lord of the Manor's deer park, with the opening of the railway station at its western end Park Street became a busy thoroughfare lined with shops and pubs. The east end of Park Street has been dominated by Lloyds Bank's handsome premises since 1904. The beehive bas-relief (symbolising the rewards of saving) is one of the town's most attractive pieces of sculpture. The 'Victorian' building opposite Lloyds is in fact a replica built in the 1980s.

After the Fire. E.T.Holden & Sons Leather Works.

E.T. Holden & Son, Tanners, Curriers and Japanners. Established 1850. Patent Leather of all colours for Home & Export. Leather Merchants. Hogskins specially prepared for Saddlery, Upholstery and Bookbinding. Manufacturers of Leather suitable for Saddle, Harness, Bridle, Brace, Belt & Pocket Book. Park Street, Walsall. J.Kirby & Sons Ltd, Publishers, Walsall.

Park Street (II)

Hidden at the rear of many of the shops and pubs lining Park Street were a number of workshops and factories. The largest of these was E. T. Holden's tannery, which lay at the rear of the New Inns. Tannery buildings became saturated with fats and greases over time and fire was a constant hazard. The image shown here records the aftermath of a fire in January 1908, which gutted much of the building. The site is now part of the Saddlers' Shopping Centre.

Park Street (III)

Trolleybus wires line Park Street in this view dating from the 1950s. Today Park Street has been pedestrianised. The trolleybuses have gone, but Woolworth's attractive Art Deco frontage, complete with typical lion masks and zigzag motifs, has happily survived.

Butler Bros, Park Street

Messrs Butler Brothers were manufacturers of high-quality riding saddles. The crowded and somewhat ramshackle working conditions seen in this photograph of around 1930 were typical of the trade. Saddle 'trees' and partly made saddles can be seen hanging from the walls. The site of this workshop has long since been redeveloped, but the name Butler's Passage survives as a reminder of its former location.

Park Street

The roofscape of Her Majesty's Theatre provides foreground interest in this unusual view of the junction of Park Street and Stafford Street dating from the late 1920s. The shops include Melia's, grocer's; E. James Ltd, pork butcher; and R. Holyland, pawnbroker. This section of Park Street was largely redeveloped in the 1960s and early '70s.

Walsall Station

The railway station was of tremendous importance to the local economy and at one point was handling over a thousand trains a day. Having been built close to the Walsall Brook, it was subject to occasional inundations, as seen here. The station was redeveloped in 1978–79, becoming, in the words of one writer, 'little more than a glorified concrete passenger halt'. Fortunately it has since been much improved.

May Day, Short Street

The grid of streets south-west of Walsall station, lying between railway and canal, was home to some of Walsall's poorest families. Here we see the horse and cart of Tommy Hartshorne, coal merchant, decorated in readiness for a May Day horse parade in around 1930. Today the area forms a large trading estate. The colour image shows May Day decorations from the *Equine Album*, a splendid catalogue produced by the Walsall saddlers Hampson & Scott in around 1900.

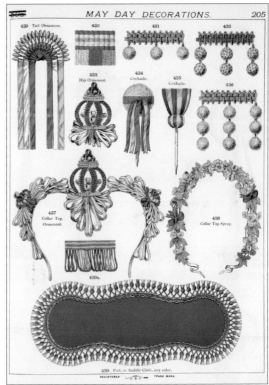

The Grand Theatre, Park Street

This theatre was built in 1890 on the site of an earlier theatre, the Gaiety. Although few people would describe it as beautiful, the façade certainly had great character. In common with many theatres, it struggled once the 'talkies' were introduced, and, like Her Majesty's Theatre nearby, it was eventually converted into a cinema, before burning down in 1939. The canopy of Walsall station can be seen on the left.

Marsh Street

The Marsh Lane district of the town was once notorious for brothels and ale houses. These were cleared in the 1870s and replaced with more respectable businesses. D. Mason & Sons was one of the town's largest leather companies, producing a vast range of leather goods for export around the globe. More recently, it was the home of Strand Leathergoods. The author remembers seeing staff working flat out completing orders for the luxury leathergoods company Mulberry on a visit in the late 1980s.

Her Majesty's Theatre

This theatre opened at Town End Bank in 1900 and during its brief life was one of Walsall's most spectacular buildings. It could accommodate an audience of up to 2,000 people, and saw performances from some of the leading artistes of the day, including Lillie Langtry and Harry Lauder. A cinema was built on the site after 1937. The large shop that replaced it will be remembered as Woolworth's for many years to come.

Wolverhampton Street

In this view, dating from 1985, the cinema that replaced Her Majesty's Theatre can still be seen. On the left are the fine premises of John More & Co., another of the leather manufacturers for which the town is celebrated. The triple-arched entrance was unique among the town's leather factories. The area has been comprehensively redeveloped for a retail park, although the 'Leather Shop' seen in the earlier image (originally built as a pawnbroker's) has survived.

Stafford Street

A successful co-operative society was founded in Walsall in 1886. The society played an important role in the lives of many working-class families, not only as a supplier of affordable goods of reliable quality, but also through its social and educational activities, and as an enlightened employer. This photograph of around 1910 shows the society's grocery store and butcher's shop at 242–43 Stafford Street. The site is now a car park, but the nearby Prince Blucher pub remains.

Stafford Street

Ideal image versus reality: Mrs
Emily Fellows and a neighbour
mangle-washing in a court
off Stafford Street in the
1940s. Most of these crowded
courts, with shared water taps
and toilets, were eventually
condemned by the council, and
the residents were rehoused.
Servis began manufacturing
washing machines in nearby
Darlaston in 1929. With the
rise in demand for 'white
goods' after the war, the brand
became a household name, but,
following its purchase by an
Italian company, Servis finally
closed its Darlaston factory in
October 2008. The advert shown
here dates from 1954.

New! Sensational!

Servis

POWERGLIDE

SERVIS 'POWERGLIDE'. In this sensational new washer SERVIS introduce Britain's
first washer with the fabulous feature every woman wants . . . *foot controlled* power wringing.
'POWERGLIDE' means *double safety*—both hands free to fold and feed, you stop or go at
the touch of a toe—and the rollers spring apart with a flick for easy cleaning. Only
SERVIS 'POWERGLIDE' has this brilliant new feature—plus BOILING, WASHING,
AUTO-EMPTYING. Colour too! Only 61 gns. tax paid (with heater 6 gns. extra).

SERVIS ELECTRIC WASHERS (DEPT. 11.G.) DARLASTON, S. STAFFS.

School Street, Wisemore

George and Marie Pelari proudly show off their fleet of ice cream carts in a photograph taken around 1905. The Pelaris came to England from Italy and established a successful ice cream and confectionary business. The photograph seems to have been taken in School Street, off Wisemore, which was eventually absorbed into the campus of Walsall Technical College. The lower image shows the college being demolished in 2009, in preparation for a new Tesco store. (*Photograph above courtesy of Mr Sanders*)

Walsall Leather Museum, Wisemore

In the mid-1980s Walsall Council took the imaginative decision to renovate an important late-Victorian leatherworking complex, typical of many that once stood in the town. The buildings were reopened by HRH The Princess Royal in 1988 as the Leather Museum and Leathergoods Training Centre. The images show the building before and after renovation. The museum has since won numerous awards for its educational work.

Lichfield Street

In the Edwardian era, the southern end of Lichfield Street emerged as Walsall's unofficial civic quarter, housing a number of important public buildings. The public baths of 1896 were followed by the magnificent Council House of 1902–05, the Town Hall of 1903, and the Carnegie Library of 1906, all designed by James Gibson.

The Council House

Walsall's Council House, built in 1902–05, reflects the intense pride in the town of the men who ran the Edwardian corporation. The local saddlery and harness trade was at its zenith, Walsall products were being exported around the world, and the borough's population had increased ninefold over the past century. The councillors demanded, and got, a fine building. The highly accomplished sculptures decorating the main façade were designed by Henry Fehr.

A Bird's-Eye View

St Matthew's church soars above the town in this photograph of about 1905, taken from the newly-completed tower of the Council House. Two of the town's largest saddlery factories, the Argent Works of Overton & Co. and the London Saddlery Works of John Leckie & Co., can be seen immediately below the church, in Goodall Street. The contemporary photograph shows the view from the balcony of the New Art Gallery, opened in February 2000.

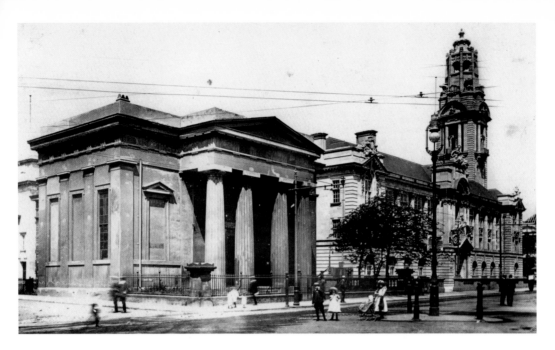

Walsall's First Library

The town's first purpose-built library was erected in 1830–31 to an elegant Grecian design. It was a subscription library but evidently struggled to make a profit, and later the building became a suitably imposing home for the County Court. It survives, minus its attractive forecourt railings, and is today in use as a pub.

Walsall's First Free Library

The first free library was opened in Goodall Street in 1859. Thanks to the generosity of the philanthropic steel magnate Andrew Carnegie, the larger replacement building seen here was opened in Lichfield Street in 1906. The Baroque style of the building complements the Council House next door.

Gala Baths

Walsall's public baths opened in 1896, and contained swimming baths, slipper baths and a suite of Turkish baths. In 1930, towels could be hired at a penny a time, and costumes for tuppence. Today the original driveway to the baths has become Tower Street, and the gardens have disappeared beneath the Central Library. The baths themselves were completely rebuilt in 1960–61. (*Brochure image courtesy of Walsall Local History Centre*)

St George's Church, Persehouse Street

As Walsall's Victorian population rose, more places of worship were opened to serve the newly built neighbourhoods. St George's church, built in 1873–75, lasted for just ninety years, until dwindling attendances led to its merger with St Paul's church and eventual demolition. The name of a nearby housing development, St George's Court, serves as a reminder of its existence.

Lower Forster Street

A group of local residents celebrate the Silver Jubilee of King George V in 1935. The building immediately behind them is the Globe Works of Jabez Cliff & Co., where many of the adults in the photograph would have been employed as saddle-makers or stitchers. Under the dynamic leadership of Jabez (later Sir Jabez) Cliff Tibbits, the company became one of the best-known saddlery manufacturers in Europe. Today this important landmark building stands empty, its future uncertain.

Queen Mary's High School, Lichfield Street

As its name indicates, Queen Mary's is a Tudor foundation, although the present building mostly dates from 1850 and later. Its resemblance to Walsall's original railway station is not a coincidence – the same architect designed both buildings. The site now operates as a girls' school, with a mixed sixth form. The contemporary view shows the recently completed Arboretum junction in the foreground, part of Walsall's new ring road.

Mellish Road Church, Lichfield Street
Built by the Wesleyans in 1908–10, the church was well used by the surrounding community until disaster struck in 1992 – large cracks appeared in the walls. The church was later sold and has stood derelict ever since. Further damage from arson in 2008 has made the building a sad shadow of its former self.

Entrance to Arboretum, Walsall.

The Arboretum (I)

The clock tower entrance is one of the
original structures surviving from the
opening of the Arboretum in 1874.
In this postcard of around 1910, the
lodges at either side of the entrance
have almost disappeared behind a
luxuriant growth of creeper. The
narrow entrance to Denmark Road
shown in the earlier image has long
since vanished, to be incorporated
into what is today one of the busiest
road junctions in the borough.

The Arboretum (II)

In this aerial photograph dating from the 1930s, the outline of the main lake is clearly visible and with some patience other features such as the boat house and the clock tower can be identified. Ward Street, today little more than a cul-de-sac, is the prominent street immediately to the south of the lake, and was once the main road to Lichfield. The lower image shows the Arboretum flooded by the Holbrook, in 2009.

The Arboretum (III)

When first opened, the Arboretum was run by a private company, the Walsall Arboretum & Lake Company. The company failed to make a profit, and in 1884 the Walsall Corporation bought out the freehold and abolished the entrance charge, making it freely accessible to everyone. It has been hugely popular ever since. A guidebook of 1932 commented, 'The Arboretum is Walsall's choicest beauty spot. The flower gardens are a joy, the lake, with its boats and its water fowl, the greenhouses, the tennis courts, the bowling greens, the bathing pool, the tea house and rose gardens combine to charm all who give themselves time to see the beauty of the place.'

ARBORETUM WALSALL, SHOWING GRAMMAR SCHOOL

E.T.W.

The Arboretum (IV)

In this unusual view looking west from Arboretum Road in around 1905, the clock tower and the grammar school are clearly visible. The young beech saplings seen in the foreground are now mature trees, making it impossible to take the same view today. The lower image shows the Holbrook, a favourite haunt of kingfishers and grey wagtails. For many centuries this small stream marked the boundary between Rushall and Walsall parishes. In 1286, the reign of King Edward I, it is recorded as the southern boundary of the Royal Forest of Carnock. Later it became a vital source of water for the town's tanneries.

The Arboretum (V)

A new bandstand, made by Walter MacFarlane & Co. of Glasgow, was erected in 1924. Concerts were a regular and well-supported feature of the summer programme. Another of the original features of the Arboretum, dating from 1874, is the boat house. Boating ceased in the 1990s, but the boat house has recently been Grade II-listed and is currently being restored as part of a Lottery-funded restoration scheme.

The Arboretum (VI)

Before the Arboretum was built, the area was a worked-out limestone quarry that flooded once working stopped in the 1840s. The friable nature of the stone can clearly be seen in the upper photograph. It was a poor-quality building stone and was mainly used for mortar and as a flux for removing impurities in iron smelting. In the contemporary photograph part of Victoria Terrace, built in the 1850s, can be seen perched above the little lake.

The Arcade, Walsall.

The Arcade, Digbeth

An initiative of the local leather manufacturer Sir E. T. Holden, the Digbeth arcade was built in 1895–97. It provided 'high class' covered shopping on the two ground-floor malls, further shopping on the Bradford Street balcony, and assembly rooms. The arcade has changed remarkably little and is well maintained by its owners.

Science and Art Institute, Walsall

The Science and Art Institute

This was another of the many projects in which the local leather manufacturer E. T. Holden was a prime mover. His currying works can just be glimpsed on the left-hand side of the photograph above. The institute was built with funds raised to mark Queen Victoria's Golden Jubilee and, as the name indicates, it gave local boys technical and artistic instruction. Renamed Globe House, the building now functions as offices and meeting rooms.

The Cenotaph

Walsall lost over 2,000 men and women during the Great War. The Cenotaph was erected in Bradford Street in 1922 to commemorate them. The land on which the memorial was built originally formed part of the Long Meadow, for centuries the town's communal hay meadow and later the site of the town's racecourse.

Bradford Street

The route of Bradford Street was constructed in 1831 and was quickly lined with elegant stuccoed houses, which enjoyed pastoral views over the Long Meadow. By the time of this postcard, around 1910, the area had become more commercial in character and the Long Meadow and racecourse were just memories. The name of the Turf Tavern is presumably a reminder of the latter, and despite a change of use, its tiled frontage has been well preserved.

Bradford Street, Looking North

In this unusual early-twentieth-century view, the premises of T. Kirby & Sons, printers, can be seen on the right. From 1891 this company was responsible for publishing *Saddlery and Harness*, the respected international journal of these trades. The adjacent shop, with its pioneering glass frontage, housed Fentons, the furniture dealers.

Walsall Lithographic Ltd, Wednesbury Road

This was one of the borough's most successful companies, earning an international reputation for the quality of its printing. The company produced the world's first self-adhesive stamp in 1964. Although the parent company went into liquidation in 2009, a subsidiary company, Walsall Security Printers, still prints millions of stamps a year. The upper image records a visit by Mrs Thatcher. Much of the site has recently been redeveloped for housing.

The Cottage Hospital

The history of medical care in Walsall will forever be linked with the name of Sister Dora. She was too ill to attend the opening of the new Cottage Hospital built on the Mount in 1878, and she died just seven weeks later. This building shown here is the Nurses' Home and Outpatients' Department of 1902, which was built near the entrance to the hospital site on Wednesbury Road. It has recently been converted to flats.

Wednesbury Road Church

This congregationalist church, opened in 1859, was designed by Jerome Clapp Jerome (father of the writer Jerome K. Jerome), who regularly preached here. The building was severely damaged in 1916 when a German zeppelin dropped bombs on the town. At its height the church could seat a thousand people, but by the 1960s it was struggling and demolition followed in 1973, to make way for the Glebe Centre and offices.

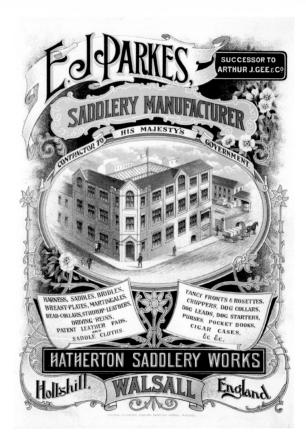

E. J. Parkes' Factory, Holtshill Lane
Edwardian Walsall was home to
nearly 10,000 leatherworkers, most
of whom worked in relatively
modest factories such as this,
accommodating perhaps thirty
or forty people. A Grade II-listed
building, it now houses Launer & Co.,
manufacturers of luxury handbags
and leathergoods, and one of four
royal warrant holders producing in
the town.

Price's Currying Works, Bank Street

A. T. Price was one of thirty firms of leather curriers operating in Walsall in around 1915. At this date the town's curriers were kept very busy meeting the demands of the British war effort; vast quantities of saddlery and harness, belts and other accoutrements were required by the army. The contemporary photograph shows Brian Hodson staining leather by hand at Walsall's last remaining currying works, Messrs J. & E. Sedgwick in Pleck, in 2011. (*Photograph above courtesy of Robin Bolton, photograph right David Mills*)

Central Hall, Ablewell Street

Walsall's Methodist church of 1859 had a dignified design that was largely obscured by a new frontage stuck on in 1929, when the church became Central Hall. The pediment of the earlier building is still just visible. When John Wesley first visited the area in 1743, he was confronted by the Walsall mob and was lucky to escape without serious injury. Twenty years later his visit was met with enthusiasm and Wesley noted that the 'wild beasts' of Walsall had been tamed.

Lime Street

The horse-collar-making workshop of E. Stubbs & Sons was one of about 150 Walsall firms making saddlery and harness around 1900. The same workshop is now occupied by Keith Bryan, riding-saddle maker. Many Walsall leather manufacturers produced superb catalogues of their products. Seen here are military and colonial saddles from the 1905 *Four in Hand* catalogue of R. E. Thacker of Green Lane.

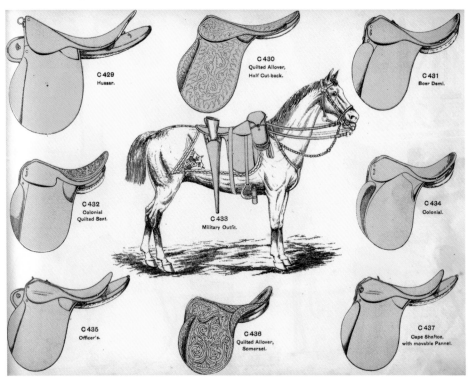

Six Ways, Birmingham Road (I)

Beyond this point, Edwardian Walsall became increasingly rural, with large detached villas set back from the road, interspersed with fields and farms. 'Mayfield', the mansion of the Brace family, saddlery manufacturers and export merchants, lay behind the poplar trees in the middle distance. From 1904 trams ran along the Birmingham Road as far as the Bell Inn, on the borough boundary, although the promised extension to connect with the Birmingham tram network never materialised.

Six Ways, Birmingham Road (II)

Twenty or so years have elapsed since the date of the previous photograph and Sutton Road has been widened to take in part of the grounds of The Elms, although, confusingly, the fine trees recorded here all seem to be beech. The decorative bargeboards of Verandah Cottage can be seen in the middle distance. Today the cottage has disappeared beneath the large block of flats known as Springhill Court.

Birmingham Road

From late Victorian times many of Walsall's wealthier families chose to live on the more rural east side of the town, away from the smoke and noise of the Black Country. Birmingham Road, Sutton Road and the Highgate area were gradually developed with detached and semi-detached houses set in spacious gardens. Despite some twentieth-century in-filling, these areas retain much of their pleasant, leafy character.

Glenelg, Lodge Road

One of Walsall's most successful leather manufacturers, E. T. Holden, built himself Glenelg, a fine example of a Victorian industrialist's rural retreat. The house, near the Bell Inn, was named after his wife's Scottish birthplace. The house and estate were redeveloped for housing in the 1960s, although some traces of the earlier building remain. The original coachman's cottage – seen to the left of the main house in the earlier photograph – has been beautifully restored by its current owners.

The White Hart, Caldmore Green

Built in around 1670 as the mansion of the Hawe family, wealthy local landowners, this is possibly the building with nine hearths that 'Mr Haw' paid tax on in 1666. It had become a public house by 1818. By the mid-1980s, the White Hart was in a sorry state, damaged by fire and at serious risk of collapse. Walsall Council courageously purchased the property and it was sympathetically converted to housing association flats and offices. It is a notable conservation success story.

Bescot Road

The Edwardian scene above shows the imposing entrance gates to Bescot Hall, one-time home of the Mountforts and their descendants the Slaneys. Creeping urbanisation in the shape of railway lines, industry and housing nibbled away at the estate until, in 1929, the hall was demolished and the remaining estate broken up for housing. Today Bescot Road is busy with traffic from Junction 9 of the M6, which can be glimpsed in the background.

Bescot Hall

To judge from this photograph, Bescot Hall seems to have been an elegant early-eighteenth-century building with later additions. A fortified medieval predecessor had stood a little to the west, set within a large rectangular moat and possessing its own chapel. The outline of the moat can still be traced as a faint depression in Pleck Park, in the shadow of the M6 viaduct.

Pleck Wesleyan Church

The attractive Wesleyan church in Pleck, opened in January 1901, was designed by the talented local architect C. W. D. Joynson. His work makes excellent use of terracotta detailing. All three of the churches designed by Joynson in the borough have now been demolished. Pleck Wesleyan Church was replaced by housing association flats, incorporating a small Methodist church.

Gt. Barr Hall, Walsall

Great Barr Hall (I)

The borough's grandest country house was Great Barr Hall, one-time home of the Scott family. The building seen above was built in the Strawberry Hill Gothick style in 1777 by Joseph Scott. It had an exquisite wooded park of 600 acres with two large lakes and long avenues. The Scotts sold the property in 1911 and it became an asylum, St Margaret's Hospital. Since being vacated in 1978, its history has largely been a sad tale of neglect.

Great Barr Hall (II)

This Edwardian image gives a good impression of the beautiful setting of the hall, which was landscaped by Humphrey Repton. The contemporary image shows one of the estate lodges at Merrions Wood, designed by the architect Sir George Gilbert Scott in 1854. The lodge, which guarded one of the drives leading to the hall, has been sensitively restored in recent years.

Barr Beacon

At 745 feet, Barr Beacon is one of the highest spots in the region, and an obvious site for a warning beacon. The beacon is first recorded in a charter of AD 957. The clump of trees – planted as an 'eyecatcher' by the Scotts of Great Barr Hall – is a conspicuous landmark visible from miles around. The nearby war memorial, with its distinctive copper dome, was erected in 1933.

Calderfields Farm, Aldridge Road

John Caunt, the tenant of Calderfields Farm, proudly stands at the reins of his horse and cart in a photograph taken in around 1910. Even today almost a third of Walsall borough is farmland. Parts of the farm were later incorporated into the Arboretum, and since 1975 most of the remainder has been part of a golf course. The surviving outbuildings have recently been converted to housing.

The Shrubbery

The great W. G. Grace played cricket on the 'Chuckery Ground', seen here in around 1900. The viewpoint is from the rear of Lumley Road, looking towards the house known as the Shrubbery. Walsall Cricket Club moved to Gorway Road in 1909 and the land was soon built over. Prince's Avenue now follows the line of the brick wall and shrubs at the rear of the ground, and Willows Road cuts across the middle foreground.

Bentley Hall

In 1651 the Lane family of Bentley Hall helped to shelter the fugitive Charles II after the Battle of Worcester. In one of the most famous episodes in English history, Charles escaped on horseback to the West Country, disguised as Jane Lane's manservant. The building being demolished here in 1929 is the Lane's fine early-Georgian mansion, which replaced the building Charles would have known. The site of the hall is now commemorated by a simple cairn.

Darlaston

A proudly independent town, Darlaston became part of the Borough of Walsall following local government reorganisation in 1966. The Bull Stake is a reminder of the former location of communal bull-baiting activity. This barbaric 'sport' was outlawed in 1835. Darlaston library, seen on the left of the modern photograph, is one of the borough's more successful modern buildings.

Darlaston Blast Furnace

Industrial activity in Darlaston has a long history stretching back to the Middle Ages. In the nineteenth century, several very large businesses emerged that mined their own coal and iron ore and smelted the ore in their own blast furnaces. Messrs Bills & Mills' blast furnace, seen here, was one of the largest. Pigs of iron in the foreground are waiting to be loaded onto canal boats on the right of the image. The site was later cleared and replaced by Charles Richards & Sons' nut-and-bolt works, itself now derelict.

Willenhall Market Place

Having escaped the comprehensive redevelopment that befell so many local town centres in the 1960s and '70s, Willenhall Market Place remains a very attractive mix of buildings of different periods, styles and materials. The perky clock tower (incorporating lamps, drinking fountains and a weathervane) was erected in 1892 to commemorate a much-loved local doctor, Joseph Tonks.

Willenhall Locks

This town is famed as the UK's centre of lock-making. Originally based in small backyard workshops, in the twentieth century the industry increasingly came to be concentrated in a few much larger factories, where automated methods of production were used. The image above shows workers at Josiah Parkes Ltd in around 1930. The lower image shows the Grade II-listed early-Victorian workshop at the Locksmith's House in New Road. It is preserved as a working museum of the trade.

Bloxwich

Literally 'the dwelling of a man named Blocc', Bloxwich was once famed for the production of metal hardware, in particular awl blades (used in shoe-making), bits and stirrups. The church of All Saints, seen here, is largely a Victorian rebuilding on the site of a medieval predecessor. The fine medieval preaching cross that survives in the shadow of the church deserves to be better known.

St Mary's Church, Aldridge

Aldridge is one of a number of ancient settlements that were absorbed into the Borough of Walsall in the twentieth century. The village centre was redeveloped in the 1960s and 1970s, but fortunately the immediate environs of St Mary's church, including the attractive open space known as the Croft, have been well preserved and today form part of a conservation area.

Park Lime Pits, Walsall.

Park Lime Pits, Rushall

Limestone was being dug in Rushall in the seventeenth century, and possibly as far back as Roman times, for use as building stone and mortar. The lake shown here resulted from the flooding of the worked-out quarries. In the nineteenth century, the surroundings were planted with beech trees, and Park Lime Pits became a celebrated local beauty spot. The area now forms one of a number of nature reserves run by Walsall Council.

Rushall Church

The Rushall village centre of today
is a busy junction on the A461,
complete with a drive-through
fast-food outlet, but the medieval
centre of the parish lies about a
mile to the south and still retains
something of its rural character.
St Michael's church and the
neighbouring buildings, including
the hall and Rushall Hall Farm,
make an attractive grouping and
are now protected by conservation
area status. St Michael's was largely
rebuilt in 1856. It houses spectacular
frescoes painted in 1905–06 by
the Arts and Crafts artist Edward
Reginald Frampton.

GREETINGS FROM WALSALL WOOD.

Walsall Road.

Brookland Road.

Parish Church.

Shire Oak.

High Street.

Walsall Wood

Originating as a squatter settlement on the edge of rough wasteland, the home of nail-makers and itinerant brick-makers, Walsall Wood expanded dramatically in the late nineteenth century following the sinking of the Walsall Wood Colliery in 1874. By 1900 the village had taken on the character of a fully fledged mining community. The pit closed in 1964 and today light industry predominates. Several works of public art have recently been installed, including a fisherman overlooking the canal.

Banners Gate, Sutton Park.

Sutton Park

On the eastern boundary of the Borough of Walsall lies Sutton Park. In the Edwardian period many Birmingham and Walsall manufacturers built large houses around the fringes of the park, in Streetly and at Four Oaks, and made the daily commute by train. Fortunately the park itself survives as a wonderful piece of open land, accessible to all. In the upper image the park keeper at Banners Gate leans over the park gate, watched by his dog.

Acknowledgements

All of the contemporary photographs in the book (unless otherwise stated) were taken by Richard Roberts between 2009 and February 2011. I am most grateful for his support.

I would like to thank the following for their assistance in writing this book, and permission to use photographs: Robin Bolton; Ian Bott; Catherine Clarke at Walsall Museum; John Gibbs; John Griffiths; Stan Hill; Paul McIntosh at the New Art Gallery, Walsall; David Mills at Walsall Leather Museum; Tony Robinson; Mr Sanders; Messrs J. & E. Sedgwick and Co. Ltd; Jennifer Thomson at Walsall Museum; the Tuesday ladies at St Matthew's for so kindly showing me around the church and unlocking the crypt, one of Walsall's best-kept secrets; Joan Whaile; Ben Williscroft, former conservation officer at Walsall Council; Ruth Vyse at Walsall Local History Centre for permission to use the Walsall Baths brochure image; and lastly, and by no means least, the people of Walsall who so readily agreed to have their photographs taken and showed such interest in the project.

A disclaimer: The views expressed in this book are those of the author and do not represent the views of any organisation with which he may be associated.

Further Reading

There are two excellent general introductions to the history of Walsall: M. Lewis and D. Woods' *The Book of Walsall* (Barracuda, 1987) and Geoff Marshall's *Walsall: An Illustrated History* (Tempus, 2008). Industrial history, which is key to understanding the growth and development of the town, is covered in my *Made in Walsall: The Town of a Hundred Trades* (Tempus, 2005). In the absence of a 'new Pevsner' volume for Staffordshire, Peter Arnold's *The Buildings of Walsall* (Tempus, 2003) is the essential guide to the borough's surviving historic buildings, while (ed.) M. Lewis' *The Lost Buildings of Walsall* (Walsall Council, 1985) looks at a selection of those buildings that have not survived.